INTRODUCTI

To tell the story of Perthshire is to tell the story of Scotland itself. No other area of the country can boast such an extraordinary variety of landscape and history. Though scenically outstanding, with spectacular Highland lochs and mountains contrasting vividly with the rolling straths to the south and east, Perthshire's chief glory lies in its cultural heritage. Mesolithic, Roman, Pictish, Celtic and English peoples have all left their marks, and the area has been at the centre of the nation's history on countless occasions. Today's visitors come to explore hidden glens, to wander through ancient towns, and to enjoy the creativity and hospitality of the local people.

This, then, is Perthshire – Scotland's heartland.

INTRODUCTION Présenter l'histoire du Perthshire, c'est présenter l'histoire de l'Ecosse. Nulle autre région du pays ne peut se vanter de la même diversité dans son histoire et ses paysages. Ces derniers sont exceptionnels: lochs des Highlands et montagnes contrastent de façon spectaculaire avec les vallées ondoyantes du sud et de l'est. Mais c'est surtout à son riche héritage culturel que le Perthshire doit son renom. Les peuples mésolithiques, romains, pictes, celtes et anglais y ont tous laissé leur empreinte, et la région s'est maintes fois trouvée le centre de l'histoire de la nation. Aujourd'hui, les visiteurs v
promener
la créativi

Voici dor

EINLEITUNG Die Geschichte Perthshires ist die Geschichte von Schottland selbst. Kein anderer Landesteil kann sich einer so außerordentlichen Landschaft und Geschichte rühmen. Obwohl landschaftlich von atemberaubender Schönheit mit Hochlandseen und Bergen, die in starkem Kontrast zu sich windenden, breiten Tälern im Süden und Osten stehen, so liegt doch Perthshires eigentlicher Glanz in seinem reichen Kulturerbe. Mesolithische, römische, piktische, keltische und englische Völker haben dem Land ihren Siegel aufgedrückt und die Gegend stand oft im Mittelpunkt des Geschehens der Nation. Heute kommt der Besucher, um verborgene Täler zu entdecken, durch alte Städte zu wandern und die Erfindungskunst und Gastfreundschaft der Einheimischen zu genießen.

Dies also ist Perthshire – das Herz Schottlands.

Taymouth Castle, Kenmore, in autumn
Château de Taymouth, Kenmore, en automne
Taymouth Castle, Kenmore, im Herbst

PERTH

Standing on Perth Bridge early on a bright morning, one instantly realizes why Perth is known as 'The Fair City'. Under the arches of Smeaton's handsome bridge of 1771, the ripples of the River Tay catch the sun's first rays; upstream, the lawns of elegant villas reach down to the water's edge, and the windows of Georgian terraces glint through chestnut and beech trees; whilst downstream, the wooded slopes of Kinnoull Hill seem to cascade into the sparkling river, where a lone angler launches the first cast of the day.

Tranquil scenes indeed – but soon Perth awakens to display all the characteristics of a thriving county town. Shoppers throng the city streets, where familiar chain-store names rest easily alongside long-established family businesses and antique shops. Farmers from the rich agricultural hinterland gather to seek bargains of a different kind at the famed livestock markets. Families play on the North and South Inches – the vast green parklands which flank the town centre (as every local schoolchild knows, Perth is the world's smallest city – because it is built between two Inches!).

In late afternoon, office workers escape to enjoy the sunshine which has been beckoning all day. Thoughts turn to evening – a concert, perhaps, or a cinema visit. A play at the renowned theatre? A quiet drink, or a nightclub? Whatever the choice of entertainment,

Left: The River Tay and Perth Bridge. *This page:* The South Inch and Marshall Place in spring

A gauche: La Tay et le pont de Perth. *Cette page:* L'«Inch» sud et «Marshall Place» au printemps

Links: Der Fluß Tay und die Perthbrücke. *Diese Seite:* South Inch und Marshall Place im Frühling

before long the town will enter another peaceful night.

But Perth has not always enjoyed such a harmonious existence. The city has witnessed many of the turbulent events which have shaped Scotland's history.

The great abbey at nearby Scone was the crowning place of all Scotland's kings, from Kenneth MacAlpine in 838 to Charles II in 1651. Many coronations took place atop the legendary Stone of Destiny, stolen by Edward I in 1296 and now in Westminster Abbey. Or is it? Many local people believe that Scone's monks hid the original stone, leaving only a replica for Edward to carry back to England. This centuries-old mystery still baffles historians.

By the time James I made Perth his residence, there were four important monasteries, and the city effectively became Scotland's capital. However, the honour was short-lived – James was assassinated in Perth in 1437. The same fate almost befell James VI in 1600, during the mysterious events of the 'Gowrie Conspiracy', but the king survived to gift the lands of Scone to Sir David Murray, whose descendants built and furnished the impressive Palace which exists today. Between times, John Knox had come to the city's St John's Kirk to preach the sermon which helped spark the Reformation. The fine church survives, but Knox's followers razed Perth's monasteries and Scone's Abbey to the ground.

Throughout these tumultuous times, Perth had enhanced its reputation as a market town, profiting from its central geographical position. The artisan population grew, and there was extensive trading with the rest of Britain and the Continent. The city became known for its weaving, dyeing and glovemaking, amongst other industries. In the nineteenth century, the world-famous Perth whisky companies were established, and today it is with whisky and insurance that the city is most often associated.

Who better to succinctly sum up the attractions of 'The Fair City' than the great William McGonagall:

Of all the cities in Scotland, beautiful Perth for me,
For it is the most elegant city that ever I did see.

Below: Colourful Branklyn Garden, Perth. *Top right:* Scone Palace, where Scotland's kings were crowned. *Bottom right:* Historic Huntingtower Castle, near Perth

Ci-dessous: Le pittoresque jardin de Branklyn, Perth. *En haut à droite:* Le palais de Scone, où étaient couronnés les rois écossais. *En bas à droite:* Le château historique de Huntingtower, près de Perth

Unten: Ein Meer von Farben ist Branklyn Garten, Perth. *Oben rechts:* Scone Palast, Krönungsort der schottischen Könige. *Unten rechts:* Die historische Huntingtower Burg nahe Perth

THE RIVER TAY

Mention the River Tay, and superlatives instantly spring to mind. Scotland's longest river, at 119 miles (192 km); Britain's largest river, carrying more water than the Thames and Severn combined; the world's most famous salmon fishing river . . . and so it goes on. But statistics alone cannot convey the full importance of the Tay to Perthshire. To travel down the length of this noble river is to travel through the area's geographical, historical and cultural heart.

The river which passes under Kenmore Bridge at the eastern end of Loch Tay is already well-established, having risen far to the west in the mountains above Killin. Between Kenmore and Aberfeldy, the river flows peacefully across the plain known as the Appin of Dull. Along these banks, prehistoric standing stones were erected, a seventh-century ecclesiastical college was founded, and the great castles of Menzies and Taymouth were built – proof of the Tay's historical importance as a routeway for primitive tribes, learned missionaries and warring clansmen alike. Today, thousands of spectators line this stretch of the river each June to watch the colourful spectacle of the country's largest raft race.

After Aberfeldy, the river's character changes briefly as it tumbles over the rocks at Grandtully – an exciting 'white-water' challenge for canoeists. But soon the waters quieten, and the Tay assumes the persona which will be maintained for the rest of its journey – an unruffled, smooth-flowing river, rarely meandering and always stately.

At Logierait, the Tay meets the Tummel, and swings to the south. Here in Strathtay – a strath being a broad valley – road and rail travellers journey alongside the river, with thickly-wooded slopes rising on either side. In this

Below: Handsome Kenmore Bridge, dating from 1774. *Right:* The spectacular setting of the River Tay at Dunkeld. *Inset:* Canoeing at Grandtully

Ci-dessous: Le très beau pont de Kenmore, qui date de 1774. *A droite:* Le cadre magnifique de la Tay à Dunkeld. *En cartouche:* Canoës à Grandtully

Unten: Die schöne Kenmorebrücke aus dem Jahre 1774. *Rechts:* Die herrliche Szenerie des Tayflusses bei Dunkeld. *Bild im Text:* Paddelboote bei Grandtully

district, unforgettable vistas are provided by the glorious reds and golds of autumn leaves.

Soon, there is more scenic grandeur, as the river glides under high crags to reach Dunkeld, dominated by its Cathedral, whose magnificent lawns sweep down to the riverbank, and by Telford's famed seven-arch bridge. Passing beneath the woods of Birnam Hill, immortalised in Shakespeare's *Macbeth*, the Tay adopts a south-easterly course. Suddenly, the landscape changes as the river crosses the geological dividing line between highlands and lowlands; though the Tay flows immutably onwards, around it the steep hillsides and forests metamorphose into rolling farmland and deciduous woods.

These are prime salmon waters. Fishermen on boat and bank can be found on every stretch of this superb angling river, but the beats between Caputh and Scone are perhaps the most favoured reaches for the much-prized salmon. Local ghillies, experts on the intricacies of currents and water conditions, patiently advise visiting anglers from all over the world.

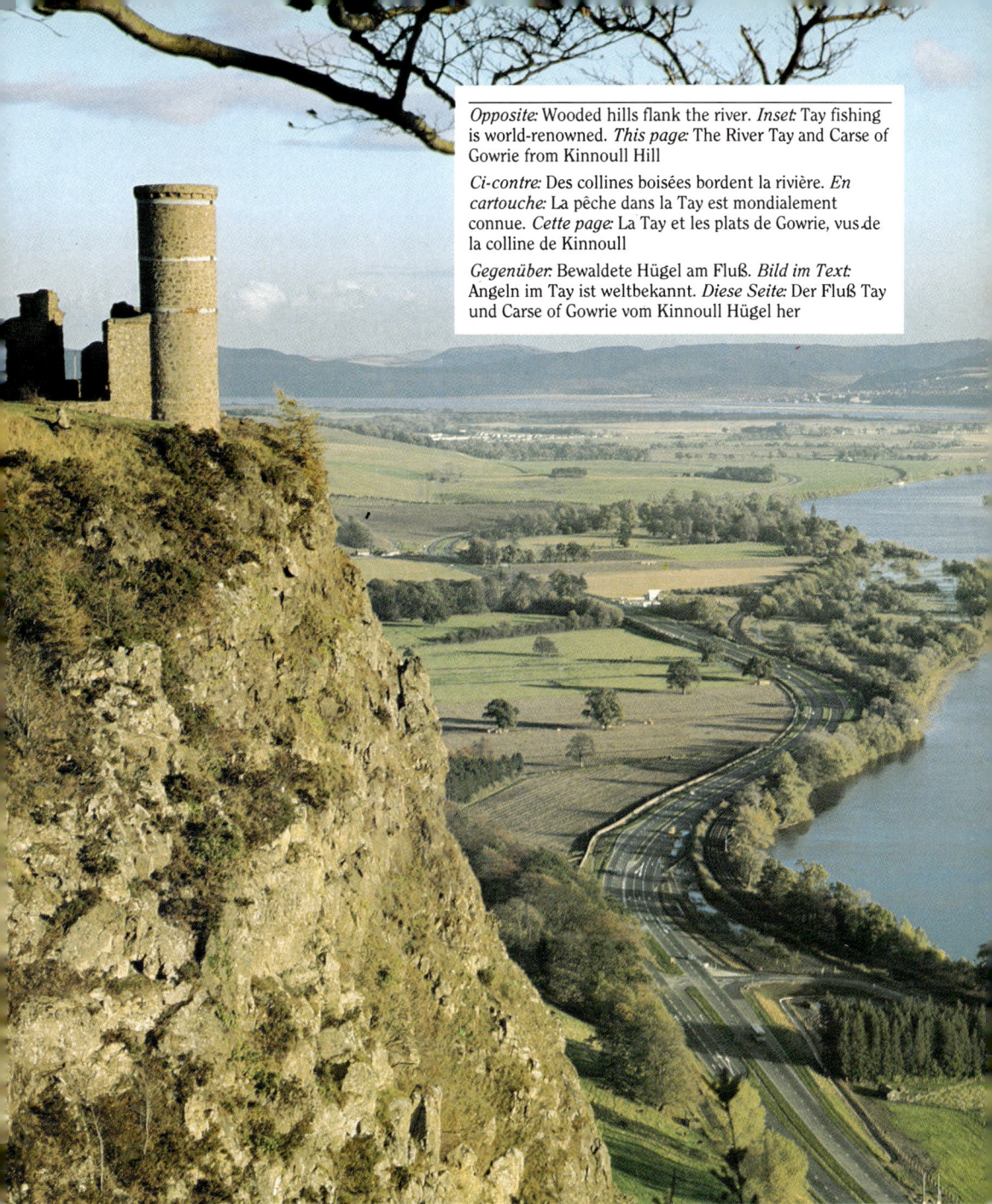

On a much smaller scale, the river's sparkling waters still allow the ancient skill of pearl-fishing to continue.

Below Scone, the Tay becomes tidal, and, swollen by the waters of the Isla and Almond, its majesty and power are very much in evidence as it reaches Perth. There is one last look back at the distant blue hills before a decisive turn eastwards under the cliffs of Kinnoull. Perth is not often recognised as a port, but access to the sea was crucial to the town's growth as a commercial centre; nowadays, its bustling harbour handles cargo ships from all over Europe.

Following its confluence with the Earn, the Tay now makes its final surge, towards Dundee and the sea beyond. Some of Scotland's richest agricultural land is found along the Carse of Gowrie, on the northern banks of the ever-widening river, and, beyond the flat fields, the Sidlaw Hills provide only a faint memory of the great waterway's humbler origins.

This, then, is the River Tay – the very essence of Perthshire.

SEE PERTHSHIRE AT WORK

One of the special joys of a visit to Perthshire is the opportunity to view some of the area's traditional and not-so-traditional crafts. An enormous range of products is manufactured in all manner of locations, from tiny one-person studios in country cottages to modern factories which contribute greatly to the local economy. And, in almost all cases, visitors are welcome to see craftworkers in operation.

The best-known Scottish industry is, without doubt, whisky distilling. No stay in Perthshire would be complete without a visit to one or more of the local distilleries, to observe the fascinating whisky-making process and, of course, to sample the end product! There are several distilleries, all of which produce malt whiskies; much of the output finds its way into well-known blended varieties, but the own-label single malts are deservedly becoming more popular.

The whisky industry has survived for centuries in Perthshire, through many ups and downs. However, with the advent of mass-production and changing tastes, several other craft industries slowly died out. Fortunately though, the skills of the past are now being successfully revived in many locations. Original water-powered meal mills, for example, have been restored to full working order, while mills of a different kind weave woollens of the highest quality. The artistry of the hand-spinner, too, has been reawakened. Locally-produced raw materials like horn, leather, and wood are all used to create products which, whilst fully functional, are also beautiful to look at and to use.

The specialist skills of the glassblower were imported to Perthshire in fairly recent times, and the area has quickly acquired an excellent reputation for the design and manufacture of fine glassware, crystal, and paperweights.

What else? There are several potteries, a bagpipe makers, metal-work and jewellery workshops, and designer knitwear studios. Whether one wishes to purchase some of the high-quality products, or merely to observe the fascinating manufacturing processes involved, the skills of Perthshire's craftworkers will not be forgotten easily.

Top left: A typical Perthshire pottery. *Top right:* Fine glassware is hand-produced. *Centre:* Whisky heritage museum. *Bottom left:* Original distillery buildings are still used today.

En haut à gauche: Atelier de poterie typique du Perthshire. *En haut à droite:* La superbe verrerie est produite à la main. *Au centre:* Musée du whisky. *En bas à gauche:* Les bâtiments d'origine de la distillerie sont toujours utilisés aujourd'hui.

Oben links: eine typische Perthshire Töpferei. *Oben rechts:* handgefertigte Glasprodukte. *Mitte:* das Whiskymuseum. *Unten links:* Originalbrennereigebäude sind heute noch in Betrieb

Lochs abound in Perthshire. To the north and west, scenically magnificent lochs such as Earn, Rannoch and Tay are found – long, narrow and deep ribbons of water, hemmed in by steep hillsides. At higher altitudes, scores of isolated moorland lochans can be discovered, while, further south, historic Loch Leven provides a sharp contrast of character. Throughout the area, lochs act as magnets for visitors, who come to fish, sail, or simply to enjoy a picnic on sunlit shores.

At the western end of Loch Rannoch, one is on the periphery of one of Europe's last wildernesses – the vast and empty Rannoch Moor. No roads traverse this lonely expanse, and the silence is broken only by occasional trains on the West Highland Line, which was ingeniously engineered to 'float' on the peat bogs beneath. The dark peaks of Glencoe gaze menacingly down across the barren, but strangely beautiful, landscape. However, looking eastwards along the full length of the loch, one is presented with a much different picture. Mountains there are in plenty, but their outlines are less harsh; purple heathers soften the tone of the moors; and there are signs of human occupation – small farms, cottages – even a school. Along the south shore, extensive remnants of the ancient Caledonian Forest can be found in the Black Wood of Rannoch. Sailing dinghies and anglers' boats ply the waters, overlooked by the graceful Schiehallion (3547 ft/1083 m), so perfectly conical that it was used for early scientific experiments on the earth's gravity and weight.

One of Scotland's best-known panoramas has Schiehallion as its centrepiece – the Queen's

View over Loch Tummel to distant Rannoch. This photogenic scene was made famous after Queen Victoria stopped here in 1866, and countless thousands have since visited the viewpoint. The forests along both banks of Loch Tummel are interwoven by paths and trails; some of these wind down to picturesque Loch Faskally, which lies between wooded hills, particularly beautiful in autumn. It seems an entirely natural setting – but Loch Faskally was created as recently as 1947 by the damming of the River Tummel at Pitlochry, and its waters now drive electricity turbines. The Tummel Valley hydro-electric scheme's catchment area includes several north Perthshire lochs, and few would deny that these developments have enhanced the highland landscape in this area.

It would be difficult, however, to improve upon the setting of Loch Tay. The traveller on the road from Aberfeldy, upon rounding a bend high above Kenmore, is greeted with a splendid prospect. The fourteen-mile (23-km) length of the silvery loch stretches out between the high moorland plateau to the south and the hills of Breadalbane, dominated by mighty Ben Lawers, Perthshire's highest peak, to the north. Loch Tay occupies the floor of a valley carved out by a retreating glacier during the last Ice Age, some 12,000 years ago. However, whilst the loch is therefore very young in geological terms, its relics of human habitation are ancient indeed. Celtic settlers, seeking domestic security, constructed small man-made islands – known as crannogs – in the loch. Two of these still exist as islands, while underwater archaeologists continue to investigate several others beneath the surface. Over the centuries, the

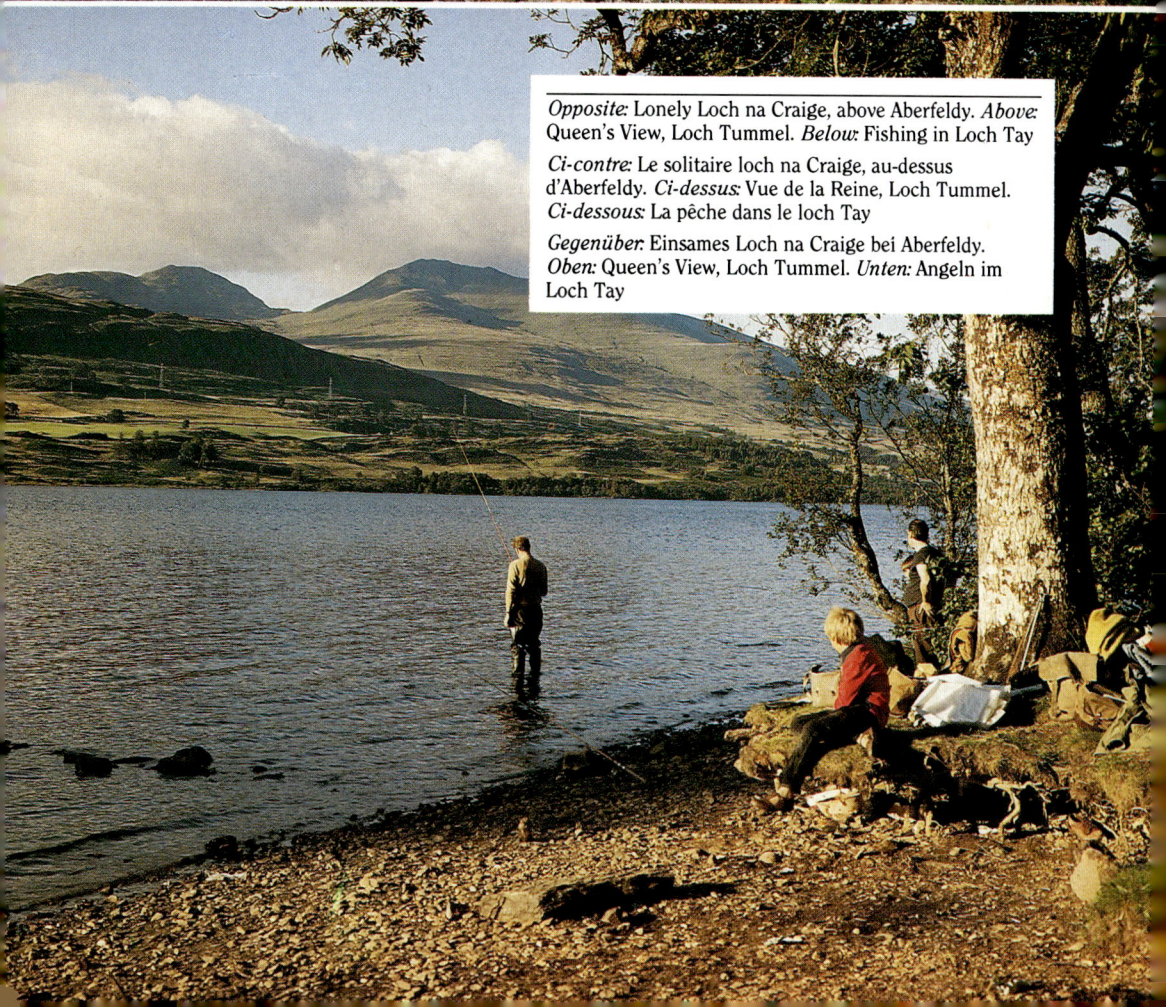

Opposite: Lonely Loch na Craige, above Aberfeldy. *Above:* Queen's View, Loch Tummel. *Below:* Fishing in Loch Tay

Ci-contre: Le solitaire loch na Craige, au-dessus d'Aberfeldy. *Ci-dessus:* Vue de la Reine, Loch Tummel. *Ci-dessous:* La pêche dans le loch Tay

Gegenüber: Einsames Loch na Craige bei Aberfeldy. *Oben:* Queen's View, Loch Tummel. *Unten:* Angeln im Loch Tay

population living around the loch increased; by the early 1800s, there were several busy villages along both shores, with thriving tweed, lint and meal mills. But soon, tenant farmers were being evicted to make way for sheep – the infamous 'Highland Clearances' – and communities declined. Though the resident population remains low, Loch Tay today is deservedly popular with visitors, who revel in such magnificent surroundings.

Eastwards now, to the 'Five Lochs' between Dunkeld and Blairgowrie. Here, in the valley of the Lunan Burn, lie several of the area's most delightfully-situated lochs, with pretty names to match – Craiglush, Lowes, Clunie, Butterstone and Marlee. The countryside hereabouts, though certainly not as spectacular as that of the Perthshire highlands, has its own gentle charm, with the lochs surrounded by rolling green fields and woodland. Loch of the Lowes is probably the best-known of these waters, due to its status as a nature reserve, but the whole string of lochs is held in high regard by ornithologist and angler alike. The Lunan Valley is not devoid of historic interest, either, and Loch Clunie's ruined island castle is still prominent.

But at the mention of island castles, the mind instantly turns to Loch Leven, much further south. Here, on a small island, was built the

Left: Attractive countryside surrounds Loch Leven.
Above: Loch Turret – highland splendour only four miles
(six km) from Crieff

A gauche: Un paysage attrayant sert de cadre au loch
Leven. *Ci-dessus*: Le loch Turret – superbe région
montagneuse à quatre milles (six km) seulement de Crieff

Links: Loch Leven inmitten der anmutigen Landschaft.
Oben: Loch Turret im prächtigen Hochland nur sechs
kilometer von Crieff

fourteenth-century castle which was to become the scene of one of the most poignant, yet exciting, episodes in Scottish history. For eleven months in 1567 and 1568, Mary Queen of Scots was held captive on tiny Castle Island, until eighteen-year-old William Douglas, a friend of the gaoler's son, engineered her escape. Mary was rowed ashore, with her brave rescuer throwing the castle keys into the loch. Tragically, though, within two weeks the Queen was recaptured, never to regain her freedom. Today, Loch Leven is a happier place; fishermen battle with the unique loch trout, birdwatchers scan the waters, and gliders soar overhead. However, the memories evoked by the ruined castle are sad and mournful ones.

Further reminders of the area's vibrant past are provided by Loch Earn, to the west. Looking at this peaceful loch, where brightly-coloured pleasure craft scud across the water, it is difficult to picture a time when feuding clans battled in the surrounding hills. Yet many tales of conflict and rivalry, involving such illustrious characters as Rob Roy MacGregor, are set in this lovely area.

In many ways, Loch Earn brings together all of the characteristics which make Perthshire's lochs so special. Scenically, it is typical; an elongated sliver of water amidst high hills – the most distinctive summit here being Ben Vorlich. Like Loch Tay, it has acted as a routeway for ancient and modern peoples. Pictish settlers and Celtic missionaries came this way, and, in more modern times, a steamer sailed to Lochearnhead, formerly a railway junction. Recreationally, too, Loch Earn has much to offer. Watersports predominate, with excellent facilities available for water-skiers, dinghy sailors and windsurfers; angling is also popular, and the magnificent sunsets will merely whet the appetite for the further discoveries to be made in and around all of Perthshire's beautiful lochs.

Below and inset: Loch Earn is renowned for sailing and sunsets

Ci dessous et en cartouche: Le loch Earn est célèbre pour la voile et ses couchers de soleil

Unten und im Text: Loch Earn – ein Paradies für Segler – hat herrliche Sonnenuntergänge

WALKS & TRAILS

There can be few better ways to explore Perthshire than on foot. A seemingly infinite selection of footpaths and trails – probably unrivalled in Scotland – offers the visitor the chance to stroll along sunlit riverbanks, venture into the heart of great forests, or strike out for the high peaks.

And, indeed, it is perhaps the superb hillclimbs, to such evocatively-named tops as Ben Vorlich and Schiehallion, which most readily spring to mind when one thinks of walking in Perthshire. But, justifiably famed though these ascents may be, one does not have to possess the energy of a mountain enthusiast to attain complete satisfaction; a gentle evening ramble beside a loch, or a short climb to one of the magnificent viewpoints which overlook many towns and villages, is just as likely to provide a lasting memory.

However, Perthshire's woodlands must take pride of place in any walking itinerary. In the coniferous forests, well-marked nature trails and tranquil picnic sites abound. And, at such picturesque locations as the Birks of Aberfeldy, the Falls of Bruar and the Hermitage, celebrated by Wordsworth and Burns, wooded paths – particularly beautiful in spring and autumn – lead to spectacular waterfalls.

Elsewhere, one can join a guided walk, hike along disused railway trackbeds, or follow old military and drove roads across the hills.

Little wonder, then, that walking is Perthshire's most popular outdoor pastime.

Top left: The Hermitage, near Dunkeld. *Top right:* Forest Walk at Faskally, near Pitlochry. *Bottom left:* The Birks of Aberfeldy. *Bottom right:* The Sma' Glen

En haut à gauche: L'hermitage, près de Dunkeld. *En haut à droite:* Chemin forestier à Faskally, près de Pitlochry. *En bas à gauche:* Les «Birks» d'Aberfeldy. *En bas à droite:* Le Sma' Glen

Oben links: Die Einsiedelei bei Dunkeld. *Oben rechts:* Waldspaziergang bei Faskally, nahe Pitlochry. *Unten links:* Die Birks von Aberfeldy. *Unten rechts:* Sma' Glen

TOWNS & VILLAGES

Perthshire is essentially a rural society, with agriculture the traditional mainstay of the local economy, and, as was the case in most parts of Scotland, the majority of towns and villages in the area grew up serving the surrounding countryside. Here were found the tradesmen and merchants – blacksmiths, tailors, shoemakers, hosiers and bakers, amongst many others – and here were held the markets and fairs that were such important occasions in the farming calendar. Fortunately for today's visitor, large-scale industrialisation did not take place in Perthshire, and, as a result, the towns – with the exception of Perth itself – have remained small and atmospheric, retaining much of their original character. In fact, no fewer than twenty-five of the area's towns and villages contain official Conservation Areas,

designated in recognition of their outstanding architectural qualities.

The conservation village of Comrie is characteristic of these small rural communities. This beautifully-situated village was a weaving centre in the seventeenth and eighteenth centuries, and weavers' homes can still be seen; memories of this former cottage industry are also provided by the well-known Museum of Scottish Tartans. But Comrie is probably most famous for being the 'Earthquake Village'; its position on the Highland Boundary Fault has resulted in more minor seismological tremors being recorded here than at any other British location.

Kinross, on the shores of Loch Leven, is the county town of the former administrative area of Kinross-shire, and contains several hand-

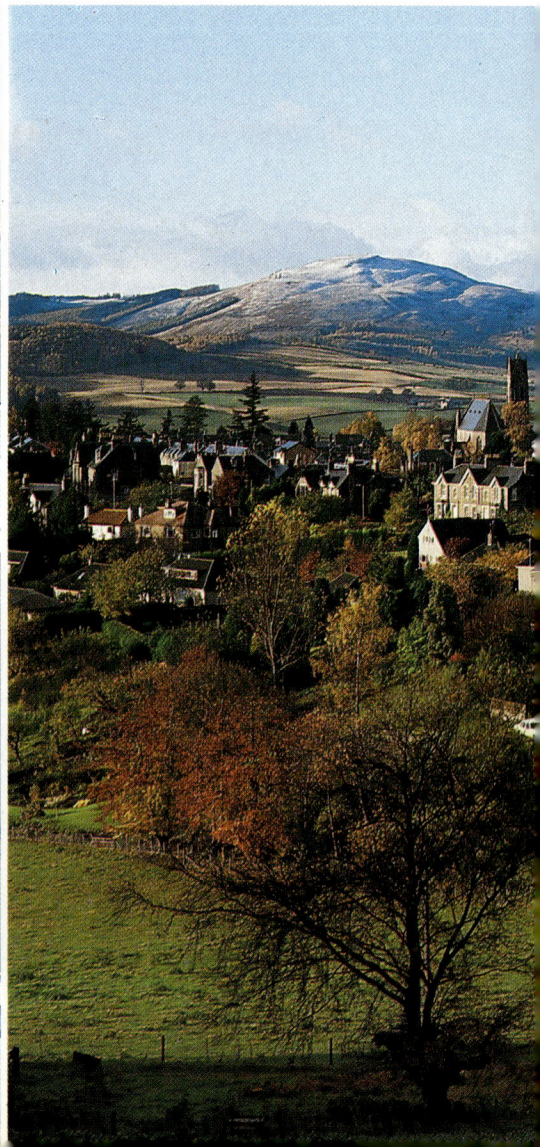

some old buildings. Chief amongst them is the splendid Kinross House, set in beautiful gardens, which was built in the late seventeenth century. Like Kinross, neighbouring Milnathort was a market town, and both communities also benefited from their position on the coach route northwards from Edinburgh.

Auchterarder, over the Ochil Hills from Kinross-shire, was also a market town, and important cattle fairs were held in the days when this was the chief burgh of Strathearn. Few buildings of great antiquity remain here, as the town was burned to the ground by retreating Jacobite troops in 1715; however, the long main street (which gave Auchterarder its nickname of 'The Lang Toon') still exists, offering some excellent shopping.

In close proximity to the town sits the world-famous Gleneagles Hotel with its four golf courses, which are laid out in a magnificent moor and woodland setting. Perthshire, in fact, is something of a golfer's paradise, with no fewer than twenty-nine courses, ranging from the majesty of Gleneagles to testing nine-hole layouts in incomparable settings. Almost every town and large village in the area has its own golf club, and all welcome visiting players.

One of the most renowned courses in Scotland is Rosemount, which is situated just outside Blairgowrie, Perthshire's second-largest town. Blairgowrie's growth in the nineteenth century was based on the establish-

Top left: Comrie on the River Earn. *Bottom left:* The eighteenth-century steeple in Kinross. *Below:* The pleasant town of Crieff

En haut à gauche: Comrie, au bord de l'Earn. *En bas à gauche:* Le clocher du 18e à Kinross. *Ci-dessous:* La jolie ville de Crieff

Oben links: Comrie am Fluß Earn. *Unten links:* Der Turm von Kinross aus dem 18. Jh. *Unten:* Das hübsche Städtchen Crieff

ment of flax and jute mills along the Ericht, the fast-flowing river which separates Blairgowrie from the neighbouring community of Rattray. With the decline of the textile industry, the mainstay of the local economy became soft fruit growing, and the town is still at the centre of the world's foremost raspberry-growing area. Alyth, nearby, is another typically Scottish market town, built in local red sandstone; its Mercat Cross, which dates from 1670, can still be seen.

But in the seventeenth century, Perthshire's principal market town was Crieff, where Scotland's largest cattle sales were held. Cattle from all over the Highlands were driven to these 'trysts', where they were purchased by dealers from the south. In later years, Crieff began to attract a different type of visitor, as the south-facing town became a fashionable Victorian health resort, adopting the title of 'The Holiday Town'. Crieff remains a bustling centre today, with its notable craft industries especially important, and, as in all of the area's towns, a wide range of quality holiday accommodation is on offer here.

However, Perthshire's best-known resort is Pitlochry, further north. This now-flourishing town was only a hamlet until the mid-nineteenth century, when the writings of Queen Victoria popularised the district, and hotels, shops and other services sprang up to cater for ever-growing numbers of tourists. Today's visitors still appreciate Pitlochry's fine highland setting; many also come to visit the hydro-electric station with its salmon ladder, or to enjoy a performance at the magnificently-situated Festival Theatre. In fact, entertainments of many types can be found in this excellent centre.

Each year, thousands of holidaymakers visit the special events held in towns and villages throughout the area. Most of the larger settlements hold an agricultural show or traditional Highland Games, which usually prove to be the highlight of the year for the

Below: Magnificent Gleneagles Hotel, near Auchterarder, has four fine golf courses. *Right:* A spectacular autumn view of Pitlochry Dam. *Inset:* An open-air pipe band concert in the centre of Blairgowrie

Ci-dessous: Le magnifique hôtel Gleneagles possède quatre superbes terrains de golf. *A droite:* Vue d'automne spectaculaire du barrage de Pitlochry. *En cartouche:* Concert de cornemuses en plein air, au centre de Blairgowrie

Unten: Das großartige Gleneagles Hotel bei Auchterarder. *Rechts:* Hinreißender, herbstlicher Ausblick über die Pitlochry Talsperre. *Im Text:* Dudelsackkapelle beim Konzert im Freien im Zentrum von Blairgowrie

local population. The small town of Aberfeldy goes one better each year by combining a Highland Gathering with the Atholl and Breadalbane Show, thus ensuring a gala atmosphere! Aberfeldy became important after General Wade built his famous five-arched bridge over the Tay here in 1733. A monument beside the bridge commemorates the raising of the Black Watch regiment, some seven years later. Modern-day Aberfeldy is a more peaceful spot, but it has a deservedly high reputation as a touring base from which to strike out for the surrounding hills and lochs.

Perthshire's most historic communities are those with ecclesiastical roots, and the most important of these is Dunkeld. It is believed that St Columba founded a monastery here in the sixth century; a later abbey was in turn superseded by a magnificent cathedral, whose beautiful ruins, dating from 1318, can be seen today. The centre of Dunkeld is architecturally outstanding. The distinctive whitewashed 'Little Houses' were built after the old town was burned down in 1689, and have been superbly restored by the National Trust for Scotland. To walk through this charming and peaceful small town is to step back through Scotland's history.

Coupar Angus, further east, also had an influential abbey – founded in 1164 – of which little remains. More tangible evidence of the importance of the church in the early settlement of Perthshire can be found in the conservation villages of Dunning and Muthill, both of which have twelfth-century church towers, as well as much pleasing vernacular architecture. Still more ancient is Abernethy,

This page: Kenmore, on Loch Tay. *Top right:* The beautifully-restored centre of Dunkeld. *Bottom right:* Wade's Bridge at Aberfeldy

Cette page: Kenmore, au bord du loch Tay. *En haut à droite:* Le centre magnifiquement restauré de Dunkeld. *En bas à droite:* Le pont de Wade à Aberfeldy

Diese Seite: Kenmore am Loch Tay. *Oben rechts:* Das schön restaurierte Zentrum von Dunkeld. *Unten rechts:* Wades Brücke bei Aberfeldy

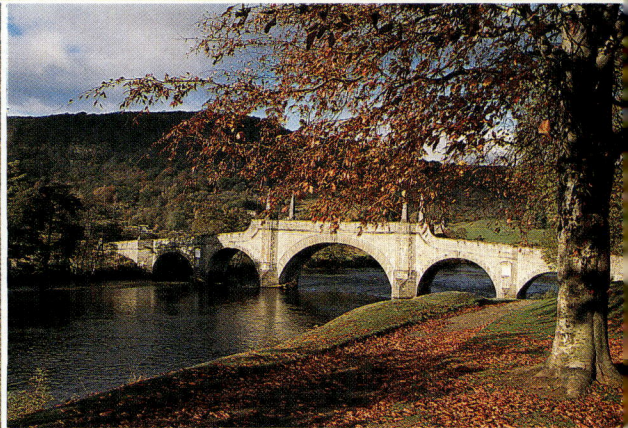

formerly the centre of the Celtic church, which retains its eleventh-century Round Tower – one of only two surviving in Scotland.

The area contains many more fascinating settlements. Fortingall's yew tree is said to be Europe's oldest living thing, and the picturesque village astonishingly claims to be the birthplace of Pontius Pilate, believed to be the son of a Roman officer stationed here. There are the planned villages of Kenmore and Forteviot – the latter once a Pictish capital; Victorian Birnam, built entirely because of its railway station; unspoiled Fowlis Wester; and numerous other communities filled with interest. There can, then, be little doubt that Perthshire's rich variety of towns and villages is unrivalled in Scotland.

WILDLIFE & NATURE

Perthshire's rich variety of wildlife can be enjoyed by the seasoned observer and casual visitor alike. One need not be a dedicated birdwatcher, for instance, to chance upon such species as the migrant greylag goose (*top left*) or the heron (*top centre*). Vane Farm Nature Centre opens a window on to Loch Leven's wildfowl, and the spectacular fish-eating osprey (*top right*) can be viewed from the public hide at Loch of the Lowes.

Strollers on the many nature trails and forest walks are often rewarded with glimpses of roe deer, red squirrels and foxes, whilst the noble red deer (*bottom left*) can be found in ever-increasing numbers on the higher moors and hills.

Lovers of flora, too, cannot fail to be thrilled by Perthshire's rich botanical heritage. Pine trees from the ancient Caledonian Forest survive in the Black Wood of Rannoch (*inset below*), and the beech hedge at Meikleour, south of Blairgowrie, is another arboreal wonder. This magnificent sight (*below*), 500 metres long, was planted in 1746 and is now over thirty metres tall – the world's highest. On a smaller scale, but no less impressive, are the exuberant late springtime displays of rhododendron and woodland flowers (*centre insets*), and rare Alpine species flourish on Ben Lawers.

Truly an array of animal and plant life to delight all visitors!

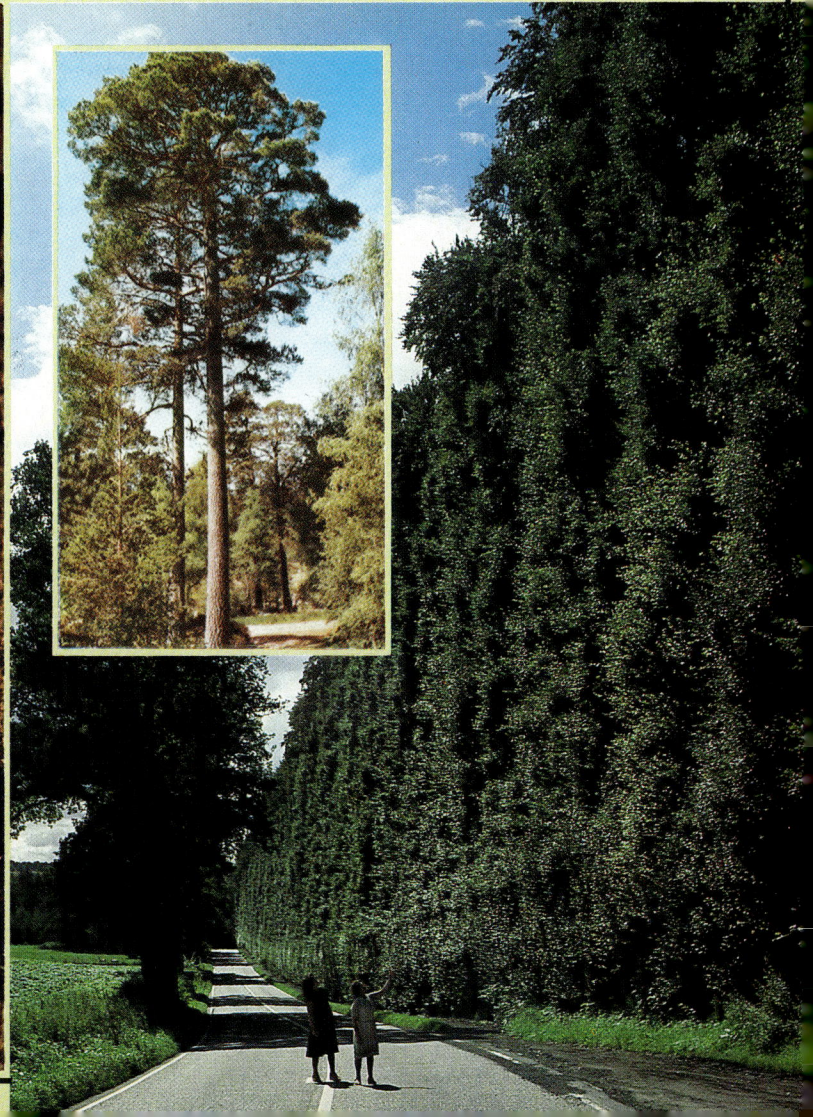

GLENS & PASSES

If the historical and cultural highlights of a holiday in Perthshire are provided by towns and villages, then the area's greatest scenic asset must surely be the glens and passes which cut through the hill and mountain ranges.

One of the most familiar glen names in Perthshire is Glen Shee, to the north of Blairgowrie. Today, the name is synonymous with skiing; Britain's largest network of ski-lifts and tows has been established on the slopes of the Cairnwell and Glas Maol, and thousands of winter sports enthusiasts descend on the area each year. Strictly speaking, the skiing is centred on the Cairnwell Pass, which at 2182 ft (665 m), carries the country's highest main road; Glen Shee proper is further south, below the old bridge at Spittal of Glenshee. The glen has many large estates and shooting lodges, and is pleasantly green and fertile in summer – though winters can sometimes be harsh at these higher altitudes.

Another renowned Perthshire glen is found

This page: Looking north to the snowcapped peaks around Glen Shee. *Above right:* The winding road southwards through picturesque Glen Eagles.

Cette page: Vers le nord, sommets enneigés autour de Glen Shee. *Ci-dessus à droite:* La route sinueuse conduisant vers le sud à travers le pittoresque Glen Eagles

Diese Seite: Blick gen Norden zu den schneebedeckten Gipfeln um Glen Shee. *Oben rechts:* Die kurvige Straße zum Süden durch das malerische Glen Eagles Tal

to the south-west – Glen Eagles, the sharply etched notch in the Ochil Hills which gave its name to the famous resort hotel. There is not any connection with eagles, however – the name is derived from the Gaelic word *eaglais*, meaning 'church'. The road south through this lovely valley rises steeply from broad Strathearn before crossing the pass into Glen Devon, the winding valley of the River Devon. The grassy riverbanks here afford many sheltered picnic spots. Glen Devon leads to the delightfully-named villages of Yetts o' Muckhart, Crook of Devon and Rumbling Bridge, which has some spectacular falls.

Glen Farg is found further to the east along the Ochils. Here is a steep-sided glen which for centuries has also acted as a winding pass through the hills. Queen Victoria admired Glen Farg's tranquil woods and sparkling little waterfalls, and, with the glen now bypassed by the Perth–Edinburgh motorway, the peacefulness of the nineteenth century has largely returned.

Tranquillity was less evident in the Pass of Killiecrankie during 1689. This rocky gorge to the north of Pitlochry was the scene of a bloody battle between governmental troops and the Jacobite Highlanders commanded by Graham of Claverhouse, 'Bonnie Dundee'. The Jacobites won the day, but Dundee was killed, and their bid to restore James VII to the throne ended shortly afterwards in defeat at the Battle of Dunkeld. Deep in the Pass, the famous 'Soldier's Leap', where a trooper jumped across the fast-flowing River Garry to escape pursuing Highlanders, can be found. The National Trust for Scotland now owns much of the land around the battle site, and Killiecrankie's glory today lies in its densely-wooded slopes, a blaze of vibrant colour in autumn. As at Glen Farg, a modern road with fine vistas has been built high above the ravine, but the visitor who wishes to experience the full romance and history of Killiecrankie should venture into the heart of the Pass.

Glen Lyon is arguably Perthshire's finest glen; it is certainly the longest – in fact, at thirty-two miles (fifty-one km) it is the longest enclosed glen in Scotland. Yet at no point is the flat valley floor wider than a few hundred metres, and mountains rise precipitously on either side along its full length. Glen Lyon is, therefore, scenically magnificent, but it was also in times past home for a fairly populous community, hinted at by the ruined cottages and mills which are evident today. More impressive are the glen's castles. Legend says that Fingal, the Celtic warrior, had twelve castles in Glen Lyon, and traces of some ancient fortlets can indeed be seen. The Campbells, whose land this was in the sixteenth century, built castles at Carnbane and Meggernie, the latter of which is still inhabited. Many tales are told of the feuds between rival clans in the glen, none of which was more bitter than that between the Campbells and the MacGregors; Glen Lyon's most infamous inhabitant was Captain Robert Campbell, whose men carried out the Massacre of Glencoe in 1692. The glen, like so many others, was depopulated in the nineteenth century, and now supports only a few farmers, shepherds and gamekeepers. Its highland lochs have, however, been dammed for hydro-electric purposes, and the area is popular with anglers and hillwalkers.

Many of Perthshire's smaller glens, while not possessing the grandeur of Glen Lyon, are equally full of interest. Two such valleys are Glen Lednock and Glen Turret, both feeding into Upper Strathearn. The River Lednock has its source high in the moorland plateau which separates Loch Earn and Loch Tay, and the upper part of its glen is now a hydro-electric reservoir. Further downstream, the hitherto undramatic valley suddenly narrows into a gorge, and the river plunges into the Deil's

Right: Highland cattle graze in steep-sided Glen Lyon. *Inset*: The Pass of Killiecrankie – deep, narrow and historic

A droite: Bétail des Highlands broutant sur les pentes escarpées de Glen Lyon. *En cartouche*: Le col historique de Killiecrankie, escarpé et étroit

Rechts: Hochlandrinder grasen auf den steilen Hängen von Glen Lyon. *Im Text*: Der Killiecrankie Pass – tief, eng und historisch

The River Almond in the Sma' Glen
L'Almond, Sma' Glen
Der Almondfluß im Sma' Glen

Cauldron, the largest of a series of waterfalls which end just above the Lednock's confluence with the Earn at Comrie. Overlooking the rapids, high on a wooded hill, is the Melville Monument, erected in honour of Henry Dundas, the late-eighteenth-century politician nicknamed 'the uncrowned King of Scotland'. Just to the east lies Glen Turret, which is geographically similar to Glen Lednock. Glen Turret's reservoir was, however, created to supply water; amongst the users is the distillery further down the valley, which is the oldest in Scotland. Here, as in many highland glens, illicit whisky stills were located, as much for security as for the quality of the water; the surrounding hills provided good vantage-points from which to look out for the dreaded exciseman!

To the east of Perth, the Sidlaw Hills are dissected by several small glens and passes, some of which link Strathmore with the Carse of Gowrie. The south-facing 'Braes of the Carse' contain several secluded hamlets, such as Knapp, Pitroddie and Rait, discreetly concealed in deep little folds. A number of these passes were guarded by castles; some are no longer standing, like Baledgarno and Kilspindie, but Fingask and Kinnaird Castles are still prominent.

But the smallest valley of all – at least in name – is the Sma' Glen between Crieff and Aberfeldy. This popular beauty spot is really a glen within a glen, forming part of Glen Almond. Though famed principally for its dramatic scenery, the Sma' Glen is another historic routeway.

In the eighteenth century, General Wade constructed one of his famed military roads through the glen, to facilitate the movement of government troops brought into the Highlands to suppress Jacobite rebellion. Ironically, following the failure of the 1745 Rising, Bonnie Prince Charlie led his retreating army north-wards along this section of Wade's route. The modern road takes a similar course to Wade's, but, where they diverge, the original can often clearly be seen, usually a little higher above the narrow valley floor.

The scenic qualities of these glens and passes may well have been uppermost in the mind of Sir Walter Scott when he wrote:

If an intelligent stranger were asked to describe the most varied and most beautiful province in Scotland, it is probable that he would name the County of Perth.

It is hoped that this brief pictorial tour through Perthshire will have helped to lead many more visitors to the same conclusion.